a gift for: _____

from: _____

DADDY'S GIRL

Published by Sellers Publishing, Inc.
Copyright © 2011 Sellers Publishing, Inc.
Photography © 2011 Kendra Dew
All rights reserved.

Edited by Robin Haywood

161 John Roberts Road, South Portland, Maine 04106
Visit our Web site: www.sellerspublishing.com
E-mail: rsp@rsvp.com

ISBN: 13: 978-1-4162-0626-2

10 9 8 7 6 5 4 3 2

Printed and bound in China.

DADDY'S GIRL

Dad, You Mean Everything to Me

PHOTOGRAPHS BY KENDRA DEW

SELLERS
PUBLISHING

*Dad, you mean
everything to me.*

*There will always
be a place for you
deep in my heart.*

You are the light that has guided my way.

*You told me there was
no place I couldn't go,*

and together we set
out to touch the sky.

A day doesn't go by that I don't think of you and everything you taught me:

to take care of my garden,

to protect the fragile,

*and to always be
ready to lend a hand.*

*You taught me how
to find my own way*

and encouraged me
to be myself.

From you, Dad, I learned the importance of kindness to others

*even if he happens
to be a frog!*

You tell the world's best jokes,

and I share your delight in laughter.

*You loved me even though
I wasn't always nice.*

You made sure I knew how to dance

and how to follow the music.

You displayed my artwork everywhere!

*You are my
biggest cheerleader,*

my greatest teacher,

my confidante,

and a mighty fierce competitor!

I learned many important things from you, Dad:

how to cool off
on a summer's day,

how to dream big,

fashion Himself according to our vanity, ideas, or preferences. Obedience is what He requires—and not partial obedience, but obedience that is completely devoted to Him and to doing what He commands. Obeying God needs to be a priority for everyone who desires to know and please Him.

OBEDIENCE IS WHAT GOD ASKS OF US. OBEDIENCE SHOULD BE A PRIORITY FOR ANYONE WHO DESIRES TO KNOW GOD AND PLEASE HIM.

Is it always the right choice? Absolutely and with no exceptions. Jesus said, "If anyone loves me, he will obey my teaching. My Father will love him, and we will come to him and make our home with him" (John 14:23 NIV). There is an important footnote to obedience: it always leads to blessing. No matter what is required, when you do the right thing from God's perspective, He is going to bless you. Instead of feeling a sense of dread and anxiety, you will have a sense of confidence and quiet, residing peace. You can do many things to honor God, but the one thing that He looks for is your willingness to obey.

I always tell young adults and older believers as well, "Obey God and watch Him work!"

*and what a good friend
a dog can be.*

Thanks for always being there and reminding me of what's important.